A NEW *Birth* OF FREEDOM

BRANDAN CURTIS HADLOCK

ISBN: 9798676326746

The author would love to hear from his readers.
Please email Committed@FireOfFreedom.com.

Disclaimer: Many of these thoughts are the thoughts of others. I cannot claim originality on the whole, and it would be impractical to try to name every person I have listened to or every author I have read. But these thoughts have become part of me for I share the love of freedom burning in the hearts of those who expressed them before I did.

It is rather for us to be here dedicated to the great task remaining before us -- that from these honored dead we take increased devotion to that cause for which they gave the last full measure of devotion -- that we here highly resolve that these dead shall not have died in vain -- that this nation, under God, shall have a new birth of freedom -- and that government of the people, by the people, for the people, shall not perish from the earth.

ABRAHAM LINCOLN
Address at Gettysburg
November 19, 1863

Contents

Part 2:

Part 3:

PART I

A New Birth of Freedom

"Providence has been pleased to give this one connected country, to one united people … and it appears as if it was the design of Providence, that an inheritance so proper and convenient for a band of brethren, united to each other by the strongest ties, should never be split into a number of unsocial, jealous, and alien sovereignties."[1]

JOHN JAY
The Federalist: No. 2

The great battle cry of 1787 and 1788 was UNION.[2] The means to preserve that union was a new constitution that would provide for "the safety and welfare of the"[3] American colonies. These colonies had fought for independence from the world's greatest military power at the time and won. Their first attempt at a national government, however, was "greatly deficient and inadequate,"[4] functioning more like a treaty between separate nations than a federal government of a cohesive country.[5] Nor did the states handle their liberty well: they abused the rights of their citizens; violated treaties; acted independently of other states when they should have acted unitedly; created too many laws, and dissolved laws too quickly (creating instability in commerce); and usurped federal powers.[6] If a new federal government with sufficient strength and authority to guarantee the rights of its citizens and to hold accountable the individual states did not replace the Articles of Confederation, the union between the states could collapse and the liberty for which so many had fought would be lost.[7] The new government had to be vigorous enough to protect the country while being structured to prevent the tyranny American colonists had fought to escape.

The proposed solution was what we now know as the Constitution of the United States. Its acceptance was not certain. It took a war of words for it to be ratified. The last of the state conventions ratified it two and a half years after the first state convention did. At that point, the thirteen colonies which had fought together for freedom and had joined together into a confederacy of states[8] finally formed a single, united nation.

This union lasted until December 1860 when South Carolina voted to leave the United States because of Abraham Lincoln's victory in the presidential election the month before. In January, five more states followed South Carolina's example. By May, a total of eleven states had seceded.[9] This time it would take not ideas, but military force to preserve (or restore) the union of the states. Over 600,000 people—and perhaps up to 850,000—died due to that conflict.[10]

What is the state of that union today? Are we more free or less free than those who lived in the decade or two after the Civil War ended? Are we more or less united?

As to the states themselves, all of them (plus a few more than existed in 1860) are currently united within one country. The unity of the American people, however, is growing more and more tenuous. Americans too often act like preschoolers in a playground without enough toys. Name-calling is rampant. Mobs riot and loot. College campuses and social media censor opposing viewpoints. Resignations are demanded for unpopular comments or actions. Individual responses to the government's restrictions and guidelines due to the COVID-19 pandemic are highly polarized and deeply felt. There has been talk about California becoming its own country. The cry for Justice floods the news. People have speculated about a new civil war.

Newscasters portray America as a country full of hate and contention, divided on some of the most basic and important things:

- Some people love America, others are ashamed of it.
- Some support the police, others despise them.
- Some think the government should solve our problems, others think we ought to solve our own problems.
- Some place their trust in God, others don't believe in God.
- Some believe those who regulate our lives should be free of political influence, others believe our lives and rights shouldn't be regulated, but protected.
- Some believe what is right and wrong changes depending on our circumstances and time in history, others believe in unchanging standards of morality.

Right. Left. Urban. Rural. Conservative. Liberal. Male.

Female. Pro-Choice. Pro-Life. Pro-mask. Pro-Face.

For a country that has fought so hard for unity, why are we so divided? Since unity was essential to liberty at the time of our country's founding, and since unity helped usher in the new birth of freedom for the American slaves, isn't unity critical to our continued freedom and public happiness today?

Yes.

Unity is critical.

Yet we are not unified.

More importantly, we are not unified in what matters most. After all, if in the late 18th century the colonists had united in loyalty to King George III then the War of Independence would not have occurred when it did and the United States would not have formed when it did. If after the war the people of the United States had united in disfavor of the Constitution, our infant nation may have disintegrated into smaller confederacies or even thirteen separate countries, which then could have fought each other or been conquered by foreign powers. If in the latter half of the 19th century the Northern states had united with the Southern states in supporting and protecting slavery, oppression and misery would have been the result, not freedom. Happiness and liberty require unity in those things that bring about happiness and liberty.

Granted, the people of the United States during the War for Independence, during the ratification debates for the Constitution, and even after the Civil War, were not completely unified and in harmonious agreement on all matters. The existence of diverse opinions, perspectives, and experiences makes absolute unity almost impossible. But when enough people unite in thought and action, great good or great bad can result.

Since unity is critical to liberty, and unity to the right things is essential, it may be instructive to learn why we aren't united as a people and around what we should try to unite. What we then do with that learning may have as significant an impact on liberty and freedom today as the choices of those who lived two and three centuries before us had in their day.

Common Ground

In addressing the question of what to unite on, let's state what should be a fairly self-evident truth: If you're reading this, you're probably a human being.

If you're listening to an audio version of this and understanding it, you're probably a human being.

I, too, am a human being.

And since we are both human beings, we have something in common. In fact, we have something in common with every other human being.

There are things that make us human just as much as there are things that make a goose a goose, a tree a tree, or a snail a snail.

Being omnivores isn't what sets us apart as humans. Bears and mice are omnivores too.

It isn't that we have an instinct to survive. Worms have that too.

It isn't that we raise and protect our young. Wolves and geese do that too.

It isn't our strength. An ox is much stronger than a human.

It isn't that we bond with others. European beavers and bald eagles might have a lower divorce than adults in the United States.

It isn't that we grow taller as we mature. Some trees grow taller than multiple humans standing on top of each other.

If it isn't these characteristics, nor a myriad of other attributes we share with other things on earth, what then makes us human?

Part of being human is the ability to talk and to think. It includes the ability to choose not to do what we feel like doing (such as not eating a third doughnut for breakfast) and to do what we don't feel like doing (for instance, getting up in the morning). It includes the ability to analyze and make decisions.

Humans are often compelled both by feeling and by reason. Whether we seek justice, or power, or wealth, or love, or happiness, there is some objective more than basic instincts or drives that leads us to make the decisions we make.

As humans, we have a sense of right and wrong, both an inborn and a cultured sense of how things ought to be.

And even when some of those common abilities or characteristics aren't there, even when some people can't talk or reason or feel, yet we can look at those people and know they are human.

We know a person when we see one.

And though I have blue eyes and you may have brown or green eyes; and though our hair color may differ; though we may have different heights, different body builds, different strengths; though the color or tone of our skin may be different; though the deepness or highness of our voices may vary;

though you may be better in athletics and I may be better in something else; though our enjoyments may be different, and our favorite foods may be different, and the types of movies we watch might be different, yet …

We are human.

You and I.

And the person across the world.

And in that, we are equal.

Because we are equally human beings, we equally have whatever rights and responsibilities pertain to being human. One of those rights and responsibilities is that of making our own way through life.

We feel it inside us, don't we? That desire to make our own choices, live our own lives, and control our own property. We feel it, in fact, at a very early age.

What toddler hasn't yelled the word, "Mine!" with great passion when someone has attempted to take away a toy or other precious belonging?

How many teenagers (perhaps you?) were more than ready to leave home and make his or her own decisions—to no longer have Mom and Dad dictate what to do? Mom and Dad might be older. They might be wiser (though one doesn't admit it until years after leaving home). They might have more money. But the teenager who is coming of age feels a desperate need to make his own mistakes and achieve her own successes.

That is part of being human.

The desire and the right to self-govern upon reaching a certain maturity is common to all of us.

It is inalienable.

It is universal.

It is human.

Equality and Government

Teenage longings to be free of the rules and restrictions set by others are a preparation for self-governing adulthood when we take upon ourselves the responsibility for our own lives. They are a central and core part of what equality means and of what being human means.

As adults, those same feelings tell us that since you and I are equal, you cannot justly rule me as you would a beast of burden unless I either give you permission to rule me or you become something higher in nature than I am—something that is not my equal. By the same principle, since we are equal, I cannot justly tell you what to do nor take for myself or for others that which you have labored to obtain unless you permit me to do so. If either of us attempted to command the other or to take from the other what the other owned, instinctual, human feelings of "Not fair! Injustice!

Wrong!" would cry out in our hearts.

When we listen to our souls, we can hear them tell us that because everyone is equally human, others don't have a right to dictate what we do and don't do. In other words, we have the right to govern ourselves. It is sometimes harder to accept that equality also means other people have the same right to self-government that we do, and the same worth or inherent value.

Protecting that right to self-government and the privileges that go along with it (along with our other rights), is the purpose of just local, state, and national governments. We necessarily give up a small portion of our rights and delegate them to people in government so that our lives and rights (and the rights of others) may be protected and we can live full, beautiful lives.

PURPOSE IN LIFE

Self-government is critical to living a full, human life, but not just because of our equality. Self-government is an integral component of being human and of fulfilling our purpose in life. As humans, we reason. With reason, we make decisions. Our decisions determine outcomes. We are accountable for those outcomes and responsible for our choices.

No other creature on earth is accountable in the way we are. When an animal control officer kills a rabid animal, it is not to fulfill justice or teach the animal a lesson. It is to protect humans. Though deer or rabbits may eat our gardens, we don't consider them guilty because of what they do. We don't associate guilt with trees or worms or dogs or sharks or viruses. We only consider humans and human societies guilty.[11] On the flip side, while animals can be amazing, loving, clever, loyal, and courageous, only humans can be magnanimous, virtuous, honest, full of integrity, prudent, or merciful. Unlike anything else on earth, we are accountable for the good and the bad that we do.

Part of the purpose and potential of human life is to become something spectacular, and to help others do the same. When choice and accountability are reduced, so is our opportunity to reach our potential while on earth. This is because the process of becoming spectacular includes proving ourselves in the testing ground of life. Understanding this purpose of life helps give clarity to the idea of human rights and the importance of self-government.

- Will we do what's right even when it's hard, inconvenient, and unpopular, or will we do what is wrong because it seems easier, more pleasurable, or more popular?

- Will we sacrifice for the benefit of others?

- Will we seek out truth and live according to it? Or will we accept flattering falsehoods?

- Will we focus on doing good to others and seeing the good in them, or focus on our own wants and needs while condemning the bad in others?

Without choice, we would never really know the answer to these questions, and our soul would not develop to its potential. This is because character is forged as correct choices are made. Love and compassion blossom as sacrifices are freely given. Lessons are learned as mistakes are made.

We must be free to choose the answers to the test of life.

Nothing else would be fair.

Nothing else would be right.

Nothing else works.

A Great Risk

It is true that great risk and danger exist in this world. We have the surety of facing a variety of trials, afflictions, pains, sicknesses, and challenges. Some people might think that a regulated world would prevent this heartache and pain. If someone wiser than ourselves would coordinate our actions, the results would be better and more efficient. If someone could stop others from making bad decisions or doing hurtful things, there would be peace and prosperity. If someone could force others to live the way we know they should live, abuse would stop. If we had enough experts to tell us what to do and not do on every subject matter, racial injustice would be wiped out. Hunger would end. Life would be heaven for everyone.

But it wouldn't be heaven for everyone. It wouldn't be heaven for anyone. It could not be heaven because self-government is essential to reaching our potential of living full, meaningful, and beautiful lives.

A person does not become a world-class athlete, a

Grammy award-winning musician, or a bestselling novelist without doing that which is required to become excellent. The work required to become excellent human beings includes making our own choices when there is the possibility of making bad choices. Without that possibility of failing, of being inefficient, of hurting others, of losing money, of cheating, or of doing a million other things that are not ideal—without that possibility, we wouldn't really have a choice. And without choice, we could not grow. Our hearts would ache and our souls would shrivel.

Misery would not stop. Hatred would not end. Society would not be better.

Instead, we would be miserably captive to the laws and regulations of people who vainly sought to force our hearts to become pure and our society to become perfect. It doesn't matter how wise a person or group of people is, their forcing us to live a certain way does not and cannot lead us to become who we are meant to become.

The more we are regulated beyond the protection of our rights, the harder it is to live a joyful, full life and achieve our life's purpose.

This is why self-government is so important.

Our Great Choice

Since self-government is essential to living full, human lives, and since a desire to govern ourselves is a natural part of human development, why aren't we more united in a love for self-government and in a commitment to give all people as much opportunity as possible to govern themselves?

Certainly, the majority of people in the United States have in common

- a desire for peace instead of war;
- a desire to protect those things that are most important to us;
- a desire for happiness and loving, fulfilling relationships;
- a desire to feel successful and valued;
- a desire for justice according to our understanding of what is just;
- a desire for our own and our loved ones' welfare.

While there are other things that divide us, one of the largest disagreements we have is how to bring about the good desires that could unite us. More foundationally, what divides us is the degree to which we have accepted and followed either one of the two great and overarching Influences that have guided and directed humankind since the earth has orbited the sun and man has labored to feed himself.

The First Influence truthfully foretells of risks and failures. The Second Influence falsely promises universal prosperity and fairness. The First animates us to perform our duties and courageously take accountability for our lives. The Second entices us to transfer our responsibility to others in order to avoid difficult decisions, labor, and accountability. The First reminds us of the equality of men and persuades us to gracefully allow others to make choices we think they should not make. The Second flatters us into demanding others be forced to do or not do what we (their equals) think they should or shouldn't do.

The First leads to self-governance under just law as the means for the greatest fulfillment of life's purposes. The Second leads to tyranny of souls in the guise of guaranteed greatness, security, and happiness for all.

The First Influence raises all people to their greatest potential, even those who seem to fail most miserably. The Second Influence shrinks and weakens the souls of men, even those it seems to bless with great power and prosperity.

The First, in spite of its seeming failures, is the only way to succeed.

The Second, in spite of alluring promises, cannot succeed.

These Influences are what lead us to support one policy over another.

They are what fill us with love and compassion or with hate and disdain.

They are what divide us.

Our test today is what it has always been: choosing which Influence to follow.

A FADING OF FREEDOM

At the time of the Founding, the First Influ-ence, even a burning desire for self-government, united the colonies. The unchanging truth that all men are equal and each has a right to govern himself formed the foundation of our Constitution. The question among the colonists wasn't whether to have liberty or not, it was how best to create a government that would preserve that liberty.

The principles on which the United States of America was founded made it different from every other country in existence at the time. Those principles and governing structure set forth in the Declaration of Independence and the U.S. Constitution gave us the liberty we enjoy today, or in other words, they gave us the opportunity to reach our potential and fulfill our purposes in life. They allowed us to take responsibility for ourselves and be accountable for our own actions. They allowed us to make of ourselves, with God's help, what we would.

Though followed imperfectly and inconsistently, those

principles opened the way for freedom of religion and the eventual abolition of slavery. They helped create an environment in which each person was ultimately responsible for what happened to him or her in life. The unique structure of the government with its separation of powers, varied election cycles, checks and balances, independent judiciary, and representative government put responsibility and power in the hands of the people and empowered them to govern themselves.

Over time that standard of liberty has been lowered and the fire of freedom has grown colder. We are no longer united on the purpose of government, the importance of individual liberty, the definition of equality and justice, and the constancy of truth. We disagree on whether each person should be free to govern himself or herself or whether the government, and more specifically, whether unelected bureaucrats, experts, managers, commissions, and councils should regulate our lives and control the use of our property and the exercise of our conscience.

What happened?

FIVE MAJOR CHANGES

The simple answer as to why the flame of independence has faded is that Americans have yielded more and more to the subtle and flattering ideas of the beguiling Second Influence. Harkening to that Influence has resulted in major changes to our society. By recognizing and understanding five of those changes, we can better see how Americans lost their liberty and what we need to do to restore liberty and prevent further loss of freedom.

First, as is the common nature of humans, Americans thought they brought about their own prosperity. In their pride, they forgot the God who gave them life and breath.

Second, Americans forgot the principles that resulted in prosperity, freedom, and success.

Third, Americans sought acceptance and approval from others, put their trust in the ideas of other countries, and wanted their country to be like other countries.

Fourth, Americans gave up responsibility for their own lives and decisions and pushed the burden of choice and its consequences onto others.

Fifth, Americans desired comfort and security more than they desired liberty.

AN EXAMPLE FROM HISTORY

Two examples from the Christian Bible and the Jewish Tanakh can help illustrate why the fire of freedom in America has dwindled. You may be familiar with the story of an ancient people called the Israelites. The movies The Ten Commandments and Prince of Egypt depict the Israelites' liberation from generations of slavery and their exodus out of Egypt in hopes of a promised land.

In short form, the story goes like this: During a great famine, a man known both as Jacob and as Israel moved his family to Egypt. There they had plenty to eat. After the famine ended, the Israelites stayed in the land that was not their own instead of returning home and providing for themselves. Eventually, the Egyptians enslaved the descendants of Israel and forced them to labor.

After hundreds of years of Israelite slavery, their God performed miracle after miracle to convince the Egyptian Pharaoh to allow them to leave. Those miracles included turning a river into blood; sending boils, lice, frogs, fire, hail, locusts, and flies; and killing the Egyptians' cattle. After all that, Pharaoh still wanted to show God who was boss. It wasn't until God killed the firstborn child of the Egyptian families—including the Pharaoh's firstborn—that Pharaoh relented and the Israelites left.

But Pharaoh's good nature didn't last long. Maybe he thought giving in to God made him look weak, and he didn't want to look weak. Maybe he wanted vengeance on God's people after their God killed his son. Or maybe he just had a stone for a heart. Whatever the reason, after the Israelites left, Pharaoh changed his mind and sent all his chariots to stop the Israelites and bring them back into captivity.

So God performed another miracle. He placed a cloud between the Israelites and the Egyptians so they couldn't see the Israelites. He also sent a wind that parted the Red Sea so the Israelites could walk to the other side on dry ground. The Egyptians raced in their chariots to catch their fleeing prey. That's when God stilled the wind, the walls of water fell, and the Egyptians drowned.

Finally, the Israelites were free. For the first time in their lives, and for the first time in generations, they were no longer slaves. In great joy, they sang praises to their God and recognized His power, mercy, and glory.

The Israelites had not freed themselves from slavery. The Egyptians were mighty and the Israelites were accustomed to being slaves. They did not rise up in rebellion. They did not convince the Egyptian king to let them go. It was not the Israelite people, but rather the manifested power of their God that convinced the Egyptian Pharaoh to free them. It was also their God's power that parted the Red Sea for them and returned the sea to normal to stop the Egyptians.

One who didn't already know the history of the Israelites might think that the Israelites would glorify and worship their God for a long time. Such a guess would be wrong.

The Israelites quickly forgot the God who had freed them. It happened when Moses, their prophet, climbed a mountain to receive commandments from God. He was gone for what to them must have seemed like a long time, but is recorded to be "forty days and forty nights." In impatience and forgetfulness, the Israelites said to one of the people left in charge, "Up, make us gods, which shall go before us; for as for this Moses, the man that brought us up out of the land of Egypt, we [know] not what is become of him."[12]

Did you notice to whom they gave the credit for liberating them? It wasn't to God. They gave Moses credit for their liberty.

And since Moses had seemingly disappeared, they wanted something new in which to place their faith.

That something new was a golden calf, a man-made statue. Once the idol was crafted, they gave it the credit for their freedom, saying, "These be thy gods, O Israel, which brought thee up out of the land of Egypt."[13]

Of course, the statue had not freed them, nor had Moses. But the people were willing to give their allegiance to the glittery calf anyway.

EXAMPLE TWO: TO BE LIKE OTHERS

The second historical example involves the Israelites' structure of government. For a time, God was their king. In this form of government, a theocracy, God ruled his people through prophets. These prophets were men chosen by God to speak on His behalf and govern and judge the people according to His all-knowing wisdom, His tremendous love, and His righteous judgment. When the Israelites obeyed God, He fought their battles, led them in war, gave them counsel and righteous judgment, and protected them from their enemies.

The nations around the Israelites had a different form of government. In place of a just theocracy, they had kings who ruled according to their limited wisdom and imperfect character. As often happens with human beings, the Israelites succumbed to the desire to be like those around them. Accordingly, they clamored for their own mortal, human king who would dwell among them. God warned them through the prophet Samuel what would happen if they rejected Him and made a fallen, imperfect man their ruler. The king would take their sons and their daughters to work for him. He would take their best land, their donkeys, and their flocks. The people would regret having chosen a king.

But none of that mattered to the Israelites! Other nations had a king and Israel wanted one too. So God gave them a king.

In a way, the Israelites ignored the law of the harvest which says we sow what we plant. They believed that they could plant thistles and the result would be strawberries, peaches, and oranges. Or to put it in terms of Greek mythology, they believed thistles would give them a divine ambrosia that would somehow make things better. Their neighbors had thistles. So they wanted thistles.

HISTORY REPEATED

Now let's apply these examples to the United States and its citizens. The men who had sought freedom, fought in the Revolutionary War, and created the United States government eventually passed away. The Americans who followed them hadn't experienced for themselves the bondage of monarchy nor the miracles of the Revolution. Some didn't quite comprehend how government by the people through their representatives was better than government by a non-elected power. They were like the Israelites who had forgotten or didn't care that God had performed multiple miracles while they were in Egypt and had parted the Red Sea so that they could walk to a new land on dry ground. Like the Israelites, they forgot that God had figuratively given them water from a rock and manna from Heaven. They forgot that God had "delivered [them] … out of the hand of all kingdoms."[14]

Some Americans began spinning fanciful theories and embracing European ideas of government. They were either unaware of, ignored, disbelieved, forgot, or knowingly denied what the Founding Fathers' heartily affirmed: that Divine Providence was the source of their freedom and guided the creation of the Constitution. They denied the claim that the principles of the Constitution and the Declaration of Independence were both timeless and universal. They admired and believed the philosophies of countries that had less freedom than they did. Now that the founding fathers were gone, Americans crafted a golden idol and sought to be ruled after the manner of other nations.

How could a people so blessed as the Israelites turn away from God as their king and demand that an imperfect, corruptible man rule over them? How could Americans believe that the governmental structure and principles that had brought about so much freedom and prosperity should be replaced by philosophies from a land with less freedom or that the miraculous Constitution given to them by God should give way to modern ideas that countered the very principles that gave them the freedom to promote their corrupting ideals?

OUR SOURCE OF FREEDOM

John Jay, the first United States Chief Justice and a defender of the Constitution, knew what was necessary to maintain America's freedom, "The most effectual means of securing the continuance of our civil and religious liberties," he wrote, "is always to remember with reverence and gratitude the source from which they flow."[15] America, however, has not fully remembered.

The United States of America is one of the greatest places on earth. Long has the desire swelled in the hearts of many to move here to pursue a better life. With its lakes, woods, mountains, and deserts, to its trees, flowers, produce, and wildlife, it is a beautiful and productive land. The economic opportunities, the range of religious denominations, and the greatness of its people are some of the blessings of living here. In normal times we enjoy great freedoms, an overall high standard of living, security from foreign countries, and the ability to worship God—mostly as we wish.

These are not new blessings. God's hand began favoring

this land even before the First Continental Congress con-
vened, before independence was declared, and before the
Constitution was ratified. It was God who prepared this land
to be a land of liberty. It was His Spirit that brooded over
Christopher Columbus and led him to the West.[16] It was His
design that those seeking religious freedom should come
here. It was God's hand that protected and strengthened the
thirteen American colonies and gave them power to beat the
strongest military on earth at the time.

How could all of this have happened without the guid-
ance of a higher being?

Of God's intervention in America's founding, President
George Washington stated, "Providential Agency has lately
been conspicuous in establishing these United States as an
independent nation." Washington also proclaimed that, "The
man must be bad indeed who can look upon the events of the
American Revolution without feeling the warmest gratitude
towards the great Author of the Universe whose divine inter-
position was so frequently manifested in our behalf."[17]

President Washington was not the only Founding
Father with such sentiments. "The real wonder," wrote James
Madison about the creation of the Constitution, "is, that so
many difficulties should have been surmounted; and surmounted with a unanimity almost as unprecedented, as it
must have been unexpected. It is impossible for any man of
candour to reflect on this circumstance, without partaking
of the astonishment. It is impossible, for the man of pious
reflection, not to perceive in it a finger of that Almighty
Hand, which has been so frequently and signally extended to
our relief in the critical stages of the revolution."[18]

And though Benjamin Rush and Benjamin Franklin did
not believe the Constitution to be the "offspring of inspira-
tion" or to be "Divinely inspired," yet still they recognized

that God must have been involved. Mr. Rush stated that "the Union of the States in its [the Constitution's] form and adoption is as much the work of a Divine Providence as any of the miracles recorded in the Old and New Testament were the effects of a Divine power." And Mr. Franklin could not imagine that the Constitution could be created, "without being in some degree influenced, guided, and governed by that omnipotent, omnipresent, and beneficent Ruler in Whom all inferior spirits 'live and move and have their being.'"[19]

After the founding of this great country, God continued blessing the infant nation. Under His divine providence, the United States grew, gained territory, and prospered. But the people's spiritual vision grew cloudy. Partway into the Civil War, President Abraham Lincoln lamented, "We have been the recipients of the choicest bounties of Heaven. We have been preserved, these many years, in peace and prosperity. We have grown in numbers, wealth and power, as no other nation has ever grown. But we have forgotten God. We have forgotten the gracious hand which preserved us in peace, and multiplied and enriched and strengthened us; and we have vainly imagined, in the deceitfulness of our hearts, that all these blessings were produced by some superior wisdom and virtue of our own. Intoxicated with unbroken success, we have become too self-sufficient to feel the necessity of redeeming and preserving grace, too proud to pray to the God that made us!"[20]

THE SPIRIT OF TYRANNY

The turning away from God and from the principle of equality that had once burned in the hearts of many early Americans manifested itself in some people through their growing support of slavery. There were various flawed defenses of the foul institution. One of them came from the Supreme Court. In 1857, the Court erroneously ruled that according to the Constitution, slaves and their descendants, even if they were freed, were not American citizens and did not have the same rights as American citizens, including the right to sue in court for their freedom. Moreover, "the right of property in a slave [was] distinctly and expressly affirmed in the Constitution" and could not be prohibited by Congress within the United States' territories.[21]

Other, more depraved defenses included the following arguments:

- Slavery humanized those of African descent and improved their situation.
- Slavery was critical to the building of civilization.
- Slaves were better off than poor working people in

the North.

- Slaves didn't have the moral or intellectual ability to govern themselves.[22]

As one proponent of slavery put it in 1837, "At all ages, it is the very bias of his nature, that the strong and the wise should control the weak and the ignorant. … It is the order of nature and of God, that the being of superior faculties and knowledge, and therefore of superior power, should control and dispose of those who are inferior. It is as much in the order of nature, that men should enslave each other, as that other animals should prey upon each other."[23]

The Founding Fathers had set up the country so that slavery would be on the path to extinction. Sadly, the Second Great Influence that leads people to tyranny had flattered and captured the hearts of many. By the time Abraham Lincoln ran for president, not only were many Americans in favor of slavery's expansion, they were insistent that everyone approve of slavery. They would be satisfied only when the people in the North openly supported slavery, called it a positive good.[24] The demonic strategy of calling good, "evil," and calling evil, "good" was in full swing.

It took a deadly war and a constitutional amendment to end slavery of African Americans in the United States.

But neither the war nor the amendment put a final end to tyranny and the Second Great Influence.

TYRANNY'S SUBTLE PLAN

In the latter half of the 1800s and on into the twentieth century, a new enemy to liberty slithered into America from the universities of Europe. That flattering Second Influence was still at work. Under its power, men put new masks on some of the tyrannical ideas used to justify slavery.

The determinant of power was no longer color but specialized administrative knowledge. People were taught that life was so complex that unbiased, non-partisan experts were needed to make sound decisions that neither the sovereign people nor their representatives were capable of making.

Not only could the experts make better decisions, they should make the decisions for others.

And they should do so free from political pressure. This would be accomplished by ensuring a good wage and protecting bureaucrats from being fired for political reasons. With these supposed safeguards, they would be free of the nature that makes us human and would always act for the benefit of society. There would be no need to fear tyranny from them.

In this angelic state, one agency of bureaucrats, mostly

free from the direct power of the people or of the President, could make regulations with the force of law; ensure that everyone obeyed those regulations; and prosecute, adjudicate (by trial) and punish those who broke those regulations. They wouldn't have to be hampered by the checks and balances that slow down regular government. Instead, they would be efficient. Life would be better because of their superior knowledge and pure actions.

These ideas that seemed so philanthropic took root in American society. They guided the actions of presidents, congressmen, judges, and educators. They were taught to generations of Americans. They have led to the state we are in now.

Equality Redefined

There were major impediments to making Tyranny's subtle plan a reality, however. Foremost among these was the Constitution and the principles of liberty and equality upon which this country was built.

The structure of government as set forth in the Constitution, including its checks and balances and the division of power into separate, well-defined branches, stood in the way of elevating these experts to their "higher nature" and of giving them the power needed to guide society to the fruition of its potential. The Constitution required governmental powers to be mostly separated. Where there was a mixing of powers between the branches, the purpose was to balance the power of the branches so that one branch could not domineer another branch. The Constitution envisioned that those who made laws binding the people would be representatives chosen by those people and by the states. It required that all who administered the law act under the authority of a single person, the chief executive. And it set forth a judicial system that acted independently of the other branches.

Agencies that were to be endowed with legislative, executive, and judicial powers and filled with employees not chosen by the people nor by the states could never legally exist under the Constitution as understood by those who created it and ratified it. How then could independent bureaucrats be endowed with power and guide the affairs of Americans? The answer was to destroy, or at least reduce, America's veneration for the Constitution and to convince the people that either the principles of the Constitution were wrong, and being wrong, deserved to be improved upon; or that they applied only for a time long ago and were no longer applicable to today; or that the Constitution was open to interpretation as determined by what society needed it to mean.

The Constitution's restrictions might have been good for people in the past. But those people didn't know as much as modern people do, and they certainly did not live in so complex a world. Progress and the evolution of society demanded that new governmental structures be put in place. The supposed protections to freedom demanded by the Constitution now hindered society from becoming what it was meant to become. Therefore, those restrictions had to be seen as not timeless principles of freedom, but momentary policies that must change or adapt as the world changes.

The ideas of equality and rights had to change too because true equality of all people meant that no person could govern another person without his or her consent. Equality meant that the government had to be run by people who were either directly or indirectly elected by the people, or who were appointed by and responsible to those who were elected. In other words, equality prohibited government employees from acting independently of elected political officers, and it required that the people's representatives and their delegates be able to fire government employees at will. Equality meant that people were free to help others or to not help them; free to take chances that might hurt themselves or might also bring great reward; free to put themselves in danger or to stay away from danger; free to save for the future or not save for the future; free to make contracts that might benefit all parties equally or that might benefit one person more than another; and free to make choices that to them seemed wise but to others seemed foolish. Equality meant that no person had a right to the food, property, or time of any other person, and therefore some people might go hungry, unclothed, or unvisited. Equality meant that a heavy responsibility lay on each person to freely choose to do good and to help others rather than others doing good for them or their being forced to do good.

Equality, you might say, was risky business. There were no guarantees that everyone—or at least enough people— would choose the way enlightened people should choose. To reduce that risk and provide greater efficiency, the Second Influence of Supposed Security led people to redefine equal- ity and reshape the Constitution so that experts and govern- ment employees who would be in their position for years (and thus gain great wisdom and understanding), or who had received training and could act without political pressure, would be able to protect us from ourselves and help us as a group ride the swell of History to its crest.

CONSTITUTION REFORMED

If our constitutional republic were functioning today as the Constitution says it should, self-government and government by consent would be achieved through representation, political responsibility, and limited laws. The people would elect Congressmen who would be responsible to make the laws. The people would elect the President, who would be responsible to execute and administer the law with the assistance of others who operate under his express authority. If the people did not like the law, they could elect new senators and congressmen. If they did not like how the law was administered, they could elect a new president. If they did not like the judgments of the court, they could influence their congressmen to create new laws, or they could amend the Constitution.

Under this constitutional understanding of consent, the people are sovereign, or in other words, responsible for their government. A major problem of our day is that proper responsibility has been abdicated, resulting in the restriction of "inalienable rights" and in government that is not by the "consent of the governed,"[25] but by the consent of unelected bureaucrats who cannot be removed by those they govern.

The governed neither voted them in nor can they directly vote them out. (Even if you could vote out a bureaucrat, how would you know which one created the regulations you don't like?) Members of all three branches of government are guilty of this dereliction of duty, as are the American people.

The Constitution vests "all legislative Powers … in a Congress of the United States."[26] This means that Congress has the responsibility to enact federal laws. Since the people elect their congressmen and can choose not to vote for the congressmen who don't act as they wish, they have the power to guide legislation. Unfortunately, Congress has abdicated most of its responsibility to make laws and given it to regulatory agencies. In doing this, they have destroyed the individual's practical ability to directly influence the laws by which he or she must live. Regardless of whether one thinks this is constitutional, the result is government without the consent of the governed. The ability of the people to determine what the rules of their country will be has been exponentially compressed, and in practice, influence is reserved for interest groups and corporations. Regulatory agencies reduce democracy, not increase it.

Similar to legislative power, the Constitution is specific about who is to execute the law. The Constitution vests "all executive power in one single person: the president of the United States. That means that constitutionally, he is responsible for all execution of federal and constitutional law. For that to occur, he must have full authority to direct the actions of all executive staff and to fire anyone in the executive branch at any time. All officers, lower officers, and staff should constitutionally be extensions of the president. The constitution gives no one but the president the executive authority. Only in this way can the president be fully responsible for the execution of the law. And only in this way can the people influence the execution of all federal law by choosing the president.

The reality of our current system is, sadly, not constitutional. Not only do congressional laws regarding the administrative state limit the President's ability to influence regulatory agencies, but they also limit the President's and other executive officers' ability to fire government employees. The president's inability to direct the execution of regulations and to replace federal employees at will means that those who have no constitutional authority to execute the law and who are not accountable to the people wield much of the executive power. This has weakened elected officials' ability to do what you and I want them to do. It has led to corruption, inefficiency, and unnecessary costs for government and for private individuals and businesses. It puts the power of the government into independent, non-representative hands. It is contrary to a democratic republic form of government. It limits freedom and squashes much of the people's sovereignty.

The laws that led to this tyranny were signed by Presidents who by signing them, gave away some of their Constitutionally appointed responsibility. Then judges of the Supreme Court validated the laws, thus making what was unjust appear just.

Although federal judges are not elected (because they need to provide impartial judgments), under the Founders' understanding of the Judicial Branch, the judiciary can still meet the requirement of "consent of the governed" because the judiciary is not meant to govern. Instead, it adjudicates. This means that as they are not elected by the people and cannot be removed by the people, their judgments cannot constitutionally extend to parties or circumstances beyond the particulars of a specific case. When their judgments do unjustly extend beyond their constitutional bounds, the judiciary usurps the legislative authority reserved for Congress.

Independence from the People

Contrary to a government based on the equality of all people, the current system is full of regulatory agencies at the state and federal level. These agencies have been called the "fourth branch" of government and have led to our government being called an administrative state. (Note that the Constitution does not authorize a fourth branch nor an administrative state.)

Some organizations in the administrative state are beguilingly called "independent" regulatory agencies. What the word "independent" in the phrase, "independent regulatory agency" means is that the agency operates independently of the sovereignty of the people and outside the Constitution. It means that they are independent of the control of the governed. It means they are independent of having to do what the people want them to do. Their independence, rather than being a bulwark of democracy and freedom, actually limits the people's ability to guide their government. It is destructive of democracy and republicanism.

The way things work now, the power of the people is largely removed. Consent of the governed is not required. Democracy is subverted. Self-government is replaced with oppression.

The fact that sufficient numbers of Americans supported these changes; that Americans either naively or knowingly cheered on the loss of their freedoms; that they did not pressure their representatives and congressmen to vote against repressive bills that established these agencies; that they did not vote out the congressional representatives and senators who passed these bills; that they did not cry out sufficiently against presidents and justices that upheld these laws. All this is itself an abdication of responsibility by the American people to protect their own rights and the rights of their neighbors.

Men Are Not Angels

There is another evil in regulatory agencies besides its destruction of equality and consent of the governed. That evil is that those who we have not chosen to represent us cannot govern us without being artificially elevated to a different type or class of being. They are given the authority not of humans equal to us but of divine angels. Yet they do not have an angel's virtue. Expert knowledge in a narrow field, a good wage, and a fairly sure guarantee against losing one's job does not elevate a person into a new type of creature or free a person of bias, imperfections, or political opinion.

Human beings are by nature imperfect beings with the possibility of doing both good and evil. Thus, while one person with great governmental power and authority might use it well to preserve liberty and bring about justice and equity, the next person might use the same power and authority to do evil and to captivate and enslave. He could use his power to enlarge his authority, wealth, influence, and prestige and to protect himself and the ways of tyranny and evil. People in both elected and bureaucratic positions can be hardworking and wise, or lazy and foolish. Since we cannot guarantee that just, wise, moral, and equitable people will always hold all government positions, all power should be checked and divided and ultimate authority rest in the people.

Likewise, the attainment of great power and privileges can corrupt even the best among us. Turning back to ancient examples, it was said of Saul, the Israelite, before he became king that, "there was not among the children of Israel a goodlier person than he."[27] The next king, David, was "a man after [God's] own heart."[28] Another ancient king, Solomon, the son of David, had the divine gift of "a wise and an understanding heart."[29] Yet all three men succumbed to their baser natures after being given the combined legislative, executive, and judicial power.

Because some people are more likely to promote goodness and justice than others, and because men may be corrupted, it is wise to limit the power and authority of everyone and of every department. James Madison, an author of the Constitution and the fourth president of the United States, taught, "In framing a government which is to be administered by men over men, the great difficulty lies in this: you must first enable the government to control the governed; and in the next place oblige it to control itself." How can the government control itself? Or in other words, how do we ensure that the government remains just? He answers that by teaching, "A dependence on the people is, no doubt, the primary control on the government; but experience has taught mankind the necessity of auxiliary precautions."[30]

Notice that word *dependence.* In order for the PEOPLE to be INDEPENDENT, or in other words, self-governing, their GOVERNMENT must be DEPENDENT on them. Independent agencies and protected government employees in large part are not dependent on, or in other words, accountable to the people. Since these agencies and bureaucrats run most of the government and create more regulations than Congress does laws, the people's primary control on much of government has been lost.

With dependence on the people largely lost, might the auxiliary precautions provide some salvation? Among those essential precautions is the separation of powers into different branches of government elected by different bodies of people for different lengths of time (or appointed for life in the case of federal Article III judges). This essential separation does not exist in today's bureaucracies where all three governmental powers are combined into one agency. "The accumulation of all powers," taught Madison, "legislative, executive, and judiciary, in the same hands, whether of one, a few, or many, and whether hereditary, self-appointed, or elective, may justly be pronounced the very definition of tyranny."[31] That means the independent and regulatory agencies are by definition tyrannical. Now remove from these tyrannical agencies the direct influence and power of the sovereign people and of the president who represents them, and tyranny becomes dangerously entrenched, à la modern-day government!

MODERN UNJUST GOVERNMENT

Here then is a summary of problems with our current government:

1. Disregard for, vehement opposition to, and ignorance of the principles of freedom as understood by the Founders and as embodied in the Constitution and the Declaration of Independence has been exhibited by both sides of the political spectrum—sometimes by one side more strongly than the other. Both main political parties have departed to some degree from the principles of liberty. While one side is now actively pushing for policies that directly oppose individual equality and liberty, neither side is actively making the hard decisions necessary to restore local, state, and federal governments to constitutionally sound, representative democracies in harmony with the principles and structure set forth in the Constitution.

2. Right now the federal and state governments, and many local governments, operate outside the principles of freedom and representative republicanism. As they infringe

on the rights of individuals and the principles of self-government, they exert power and authority where Nature and God say they have no right to do so.

3. The people of America have not acted on their responsibility to know the principles of the Constitution and to defend them. They have not demanded that their congressmen enact laws that protect inalienable rights equally for all individuals and that support and accord with the Constitution as the Founders understood it. Nor have the people refused to elect the congressmen who support laws contrary to the principles of individual liberty and freedom

4. Congress has yielded much of its responsibility and duty to legislate into the hands of tyrannical regulatory agencies—tyrannical because they combine the executive, judicial, and legislative powers within one organization, and tyrannical because they are run by unelected bureaucrats who are not accountable to the people. Regulatory agencies hold all three powers of government within one department. The people within the agencies who make the rules by which we must live are not representatives of the people. This is directly contrary to two key principles that make possible a successful and lasting free government, namely a "distribution of power into distinct departments" and "the representation of the people in the legislature, by deputies of their own election."[32]

5. Our judiciary (the Supreme Court and the related system of federal courts) often delegates its responsibility of interpreting law by deferring to the opinions of regulatory agencies and to the supposed reasonableness of state governments. In doing this, it gives to other bodies the power the Constitution expressly gave it. At the same time, the Court often usurps power not given to the judiciary, namely issuing mandates that apply to people and circumstances outside the specific case before it. In doing this, it legislates. This is a

power it has no constitutional authority to wield.

6. Our national congress has passed bills, and Presidents of the United States have signed into law bills that enable tyranny and that give to the federal government power to do what the Constitution does not give it authority to do. In other words, the sovereign people gave the federal government power to do specific things, and the federal government has used that delegated power to claim additional power and to boss around its sovereign: namely, we, the people. The result is akin to parents giving authority to their oldest children to babysit their younger siblings. Then those children with delegated authority turn and issue orders to their parents and even enforce their orders. "Dad," one of the babysitting children says, "you will place an extra-large, thin-crust, meat-lover's pizza with extra sauce and double cheese outside my bedroom door by 6:00 PM or I'll slash your tires." Presidents and congresses have authorized the shifting of executive power away from the president and into the hands of agencies not under the direct control of the president. This unconstitutionally-wielded executive, legislative and judicial power by unconstitutional, unelected bureaucrats, officers, and judges is often used to legislate, enforce, and adjudicate regulations that are themselves unconstitutional and tyrannical.

7. The formalizing of government away from the principles of liberty and representative republicanism has led to great feelings of powerlessness among the people. They have lost power because they have given it away. An example close to home for many people is that of an unelected city manager (who may not even live in the city) running a city instead of an elected mayor who is beholden to the citizens of the city. Another example is a homeowner association that regulates lawn care, pets, and curtain color.

8. Many Americans are increasingly forgetting and turning away from that Divine Providence that the Founding Fathers recognized as guiding and enabling our freedom from Great Britain and whose blessing rested upon the construction of the Constitution and our United States. It was God who protected this country and enabled it to beat the greatest military power on earth. It was God who inspired the hearts of men to desire liberty, and who gathered together the best people of that time to put together the Constitution and who instilled in them the wisdom and principles that would bring about liberty in preparation for His Son's coming. We need to turn to God as a people to preserve our liberty, our security, and our prosperity.

9. The fire of individual liberty has gone out in some people and dimmed in others because of generations of glittering ideas that on the surface appear pleasing but which degrade and shackle the soul of man, and because of increasing governmental benefits given to this group or that. As a people, we have forgotten what it feels like to be free and responsible for ourselves. We have lost the love of liberty. The ancient Israelites, when experiencing the difficulties of freedom, murmured and wanted to return to the security and false benefits of slavery. Like them, many Americans have given up freedom in exchange for cake that cannot sustain and for the protection of figurative bars on their windows that keep them prisoner more than they keep out intruders.

The great evil, not just of regulatory agencies, but also of laws that do something other than protect our rights, is that our ability to self-govern is diminished, which means that our ability to do the most good and to become our greatest and happiest selves while in this life, is diminished.

Light of Hope

In the guise of lovingly helping people, the Second Influence has increased in power and effect. Today, we are suffering a deprivation of rights from regressive changes to our three branches of government—changes that oppose the doctrines and structure established by the Constitution as understood by its creators. Our nation, though it still enjoys many freedoms, has listened to the Second Influence and slid into tyranny—not tyranny of the one, but tyranny of the millions, tyranny of non-elected officers and bureaucrats that operate at the local, state, and federal levels. However well-meaning and good those individuals may be, and however sincere and compassionate their desires, the positions they occupy are positions of tyranny and the regulations they enact and enforce are bondage.

This tyranny came upon us by degrees and because of the perverted promise that life would be better if others made decisions for us—those who knew more, who were experts, who were independent of the will of the people. Tyranny also gained power because of the promise of benefits in exchange for our rights. Naively, our country gave in to this sophistry, abdicating responsibility for ourselves and accepting bondage in exchange for supposed efficiency, security, and benefits. Americans sold their birthright for a pot of porridge.

There is hope, however. You and I still hold the sovereign power to undo what has been done and restore government by consent of the governed if we but have the will and take the necessary action.

In order for this to happen, lovers of liberty must take responsibility for the current state of government. We can elect a president who will abide by his oath to "preserve, protect and defend the Constitution;"[33] who will promote constitutional principles; and who will veto unconstitutional laws. We can elect senators and congressmen who will retake responsibility for all legislative actions. We can demand that the incumbent Congress and newly elected congressmen restore unitary executive authority to the President and legislative power to the Congress. Then we must hold our president, senators, and congressmen responsible for fulfilling our wishes.

Ultimate sovereignty lies in the people, but we only have power when we choose to take responsibility for our government and exercise that sovereignty. Such an exercise can restore self-government, representative government by consent, and the rights and freedoms that will allow us to determine our own destiny and live beautiful and fulfilling lives.

We cannot as a nation hold two diametrically opposing beliefs for long and be one people. We can be united in treacherous falsehoods that will only bring more and more misery. Or we can be united in Truth and Liberty. The fence between the two will eventually fall and we must be either all free (with our rights protected) or some of us will be slaves and the rest masters.

PART 2

PLATFORM OF A LOVER OF LIBERTY

Our constitutional form of government was intentionally created to preserve individual rights and to provide for the consent of the governed. It is based on timeless and universal principles that do not change. This means that they can work as well today as they did at the time our country was created. Those principles are in effect laws, that if followed, bring liberty and the opportunity for each person to become who he or she was meant to become. When the laws of freedom are not followed and the supporting structure of government set up by the Constitution is changed, the government cannot fully fulfill its legitimate and just purpose, and you and I lose our freedom.

Such is the situation today.

We need to return to the standard of individual liberty and equality that is enshrined in the U.S. Constitution and in its companion document, the Declaration of Independence. To do this, we need to understand our current condition, reassert our sovereignty, and take responsibility for the state we are in. We also need a president, congress, and judiciary who have the understanding and will to again fulfill the responsibilities given them by the Constitution and loose the shackles of regressive doctrine and governmental structures that infringe the inalienable rights of individuals; in other words, that restrict the inalienable rights of you, of me, and of our families and friends.

While we have the power to restore our freedoms and preserve this nation, let us commit to learning the principles of liberty and of searching out moral, honest, and wise people to run for office. Let us stand up for our rights in the face of the deafening and shaming crowd of those who seek to silence opposing thought and destroy liberty. Let us have the courage to run for office, speak up at town halls, and share our opinions with neighbors and our government representatives and officers.

To assist in this work, I offer a platform of constitutional principles that lovers of liberty may use to guide their choice of political candidates or run for office themselves.

SHINING POINTS OF FREEDOM

RIGHTS

Rights are what we as individuals should have the freedom to do or have, or seek to do or have, simply because we are human. They are not obligations owed us from others. They belong to every human being simply because we are human. It is the humanness in us that gives us those rights. You might say that it is our very nature that results in human rights. They cannot be given to us by other humans because they are already ours. God already gave them to us—or, if you prefer, our nature gave them to us. Regardless of their origin—whether from God or nature—the fact that we are human means that we have rights that should be used and protected.

This means that the government cannot grant truly inalienable rights. It cannot do this because it cannot make humans more human than they already are. Governments can only protect, ignore, or restrict our rights.

Unjust governments restrict these rights. Just governments protect them. The role of just government is to create a safe environment for making choices, provide order and safety (think of traffic laws), and create an environment of secure transactions (think of contract laws). There must be law and government, but these are meant to create safety and security, and to protect people's freedom to make their own choices and live their own lives. Taxes are necessary for governments but should be limited so as to minimize their impact on a citizen's rights.

Utmost among these rights is the freedom to worship as one wishes, to express one's beliefs, to guide one's own family, to own and manage property, to earn a living, and to protect oneself and one's family from those who would trample those rights. All these are inherent in the right to life and liberty.

Property both sustains life and allows us to pursue happiness. This right means that an elderly couple who owns their home should not have to pay rent to the local or state government (i.e., property taxes) in order to continue living in their own home. The rights to life, property, and the pursuit of happiness also mean that a person has the right to provide for himself and his family without asking permission of his neighbors or his city or state before earning an income. Homeowner Associations are one of the most nefarious small governments that deprive people of their liberty and their right to use their own property. Liberty and the pursuit of happiness mean that each individual gets to make choices for himself, as long as his choices do not take away another's right to make choices.

Choose candidates who believe true rights should be protected, cannot be granted, and should not be violated except by consent of the governed, and then only to the smallest degree necessary.

Purpose of Government

The purpose of just government is to protect individuals and their God-given rights to property, to life, and to making their own choices. While we must have a strong and energetic government, both the powers of the federal and the state governments are constitutionally limited. Though not specifically enumerated, there are powers that are reserved to the people. The Declaration of Independence sets forth the principles upon which our government—and our liberty—was founded. The Preamble to the Constitution states the objective of our government, while the body of the Constitution describes the boundaries within which government may legitimately work to achieve those ends.

Choose candidates who believe the purpose of government is to protect each person's life, property, and freedom of choice.

Individual Responsibility

Individuals must take responsibility for their own lives, for their communities, and for what happens in government. Though the government may at times assist, it is not the government's job to fix societal ills. It is society's job. That means it is my job and your job. Individuals need to provide for self, family, and community. Dignity and self-respect are preserved as each person contributes to society and—to the best of his or her ability—earns the value he receives.

The private citizens of America are the ones who should feed and clothe the poor, take care of the ill, etc. They need to be able to start and run businesses so that their neighbors have employment. They need to be free to decide what color of curtains to hang in their front windows, how many acres of wheat to grow, what their children should learn, whether to have health insurance, how much to pay employees, what benefits to offer, what type of light bulb to buy, etc. In order to become who we are meant to be, we must be free to make our own choices and pursue happiness as we understand what that pursuit entails.

We also have the individual responsibility to understand the principles of liberty and to sustain and uphold them. It is our responsibility to ensure that those in power act as they should act and that the structure of government as set forth in the Constitution is restored.

Choose candidates who promote individual responsibility.

Unity and Common Good

A house divided against itself cannot stand. Much of political energy is spent dividing people into groups: men, women; blacks, whites; Native Americans, Latino Americans, Asian Americans, African Americans; right, left; rich, poor, middle class; rural, urban; blue collar, white collar, gray collar; working class, upper class, elite, privileged, and underprivileged. This nation was founded on the knowledge that "all men are created equal" and that they equally have God-given "unalienable Rights."[34] We are all members of the same human family. Our country needs unity, not divisiveness; kindness, not rudeness; honesty, not expediency and political correctness. We need more "united states" and less "divisive states". Unity in liberty comes as we unite in a common understanding of, love for, and commitment to self-government and individual rights. It comes as we seek solutions that respect the dignity of all people and that follow just principles, regardless of which political party currently favors or disfavors the solutions. It comes as each of us intentionally and diligently seeks to learn what makes a choice good, and strives to make good choices. Our loyalty should not be to party, but to what is right.

Choose candidates who seek to unite people in love, liberty, and the pursuit of truth and goodness.

Loyalty to Conscience and to the Constitution

Federally elected representatives and executive officers have a duty to their conscience and to the Constitution of the United States. These two loyalties—conscience and Constitution—should come before party, before ideology, before popularity, before the seeking of votes and the grabbing or holding of power.

Any veering away from or reinterpretation of Constitutional principles necessarily leads to tyranny. Federal and state officers of all three branches of government are constitutionally oath-bound "to support [the] Constitution."[35] Those actions and ideas that reduce self-government under the law; that masquerade group privilege and government-granted benefits as equal, natural, and inalienable rights; that seek control over human decision and generosity; that threaten man's freedom to worship, think, and speak freely and publicly; that limit man's power to defend himself and family and to own and use property as he wishes (always respecting the right of others to do the same)—these are the enemies to the Constitution. These are the enemies to our liberty. These are enemies to happiness. No public official can support these tyrannical ideas and at the same time fulfill his or her mandated oath to support the Constitution.

When what is right goes against what is politically popular at the moment, the brave statesman does what is right. When what is popular goes against what is truly constitutional, the honest statesman upholds the Constitution. If what the person feels is right seems to go against the Constitution, he or she is duty-bound and legally-bound to obey the Constitution while at the same time being free to seek to change the Constitution through Constitutional means, specifically, through the amendment process.

Choose candidates who will be loyal to conscience and the Constitution.

MORALITY

We can be a free people and have God's blessings shine upon us only so long as we are a moral people. John Adams correctly said that "Our Constitution was made only for a moral and religious People. It is wholly inadequate to the government of any other."[36] There are absolute rights and wrongs with their attendant consequences. Prosperity and security come from following God's laws, not from the ideas of men nor from missiles and bombs. Obeying God's laws is essential to receiving His protection as a nation, and is our greatest defense against our enemies.

As a people, we need to do better at recognizing God's divine hand in our country's founding and in our daily lives. We need to look for God's blessings and be grateful for them. We need to obey His commands as best we know them.

For those who do not believe in God, hold fast to the belief that there are universal rights and wrongs that do not change; that there is commonality among all people that distinguishes us from the beasts, that unites us, and that requires consent in order to be justly governed; and that there are timeless principles that enable a person to reach his or her potential. You might also ponder on the wonder of this world, of our bodies, of the universe, and of the founding of this country. You might consider how many trillions and trillions of perfect interactions had to happen for all of this to be. Could we really be the result of accident?

Choose candidates who believe in absolute rights and wrongs and who will encourage people to seek to know and to choose the right.

FEDERALISM AND REPUBLICANISM

The federal government has specific, enumerated powers. All other powers are reserved to the states and to the people. States, however, like the national government, must also respect and protect the inalienable rights of all people. Both the federal government and state and local governments need to return to a republican form of government. In fact, the Constitution requires that the federal government guarantee to each state "a Republican Form of Government."[37]

While the federal government is authorized and has the responsibility to protect the rights of the nation and the welfare of the people as a united group (always within the restraints given in the Constitution), it is the duty of states to protect individuals and their rights.

In local and state governments—as in the federal—it is the elected officials who should make and administer the laws, not appointed or hired officials, agencies, committees, councils, or commissions. Federalism is part of the separation of powers that preserve liberty and promotes peace and the general welfare. As such, the federal government should focus on the concerns appointed to it by the Constitution and leave to the States and to the people to work out for themselves the concerns left to them. Proper implementation of this separation of powers can result in better solutions, greater accountability to the people, lower taxes, an unleashing of creativity and ingenuity, an outpouring of compassion and love, and a swelling of freedom.

Choose candidates who believe in the separation of powers between federal and state governments.

Interpretation of Law

All three branches of government must interpret the Constitution and the law. This includes the Executive branch. The president is constitutionally oath-bound to do two things: "faithfully execute the Office of the President" and "preserve, protect and defend the Constitution of the United States."[38] The Constitution also obligates the Executive to "take Care that the Laws be faithfully executed."[39] This obligation includes, "This Constitution, and the Laws of the United States which shall be made in Pursuance thereof."[40] To fulfill this duty to execute the law, the Executive must interpret both the Constitution and the law. Likewise, the Executive must interpret the Constitution in order to defend it. His interpretation is as valid within his sphere of responsibilities as the interpretation of the other branches of government.

Congress too must interpret the Constitution. Only those "Laws of the United States which shall be made in Pursuance thereof," or in other words, in agreement with the Constitution, are "the supreme Law of the Land."[41] Therefore, Congress has a duty to interpret the Constitution in order to ensure that federal law is in harmony with it. They must also interpret the Constitution to decide whether to impeach judges or executive officers.[42]

The federal courts, among other things, are tasked to decide "all Cases, in Law and Equity, arising under this Constitution, [and] the Laws of the United States."[43] In order to do this, they too must interpret both the Constitution and federal laws. Chief Justice John Marshall, in 1803 stated, "Those who apply the rule to particular cases must, of necessity, expound and interpret that rule."[44] In other words, applying the law to particular parties in particular circumstances is the role of the court, and in order to fulfill its role, it must "expound and interpret" the Constitution and other laws.

Justice Marshall recognized, however, that there was a place for the President of the United States to likewise interpret law. "The province of the Court," he declared, "is solely to decide on the rights of individuals, not to inquire how the Executive or Executive officers perform duties in which they have a discretion."[45]

Thomas Jefferson likewise believed in the right of each branch to interpret the Constitution in relation to its Constitutionally-granted authorities, even though the different branches might have different interpretations. He wrote, "[Y]ou seem … to consider the judges as the ultimate arbiters of all constitutional questions: a very dangerous doctrine indeed … The constitution has erected no such single tribunal … It has more wisely made all the departments co-equal and co-sovereign within themselves. … "[46, 47]

The American people also have a responsibility to study, understand, and interpret the Constitution so that they can judge the actions of those who legislate, administer, and adjudicate the law. Ultimately, it is our responsibility as the people of the United States to uphold and defend the Constitution. Understanding some parts of the Constitution may require a dictionary or other aid (such as when the Constitution refers to "Letters of Marque and Reprisal"), but much of it can be understood by anyone who conscientiously studies it. No law degree is required.

Choose candidates who understand the co-equal nature of the three branches of government and their equal responsibility to interpret the Constitution.

Unitary Executive Essential

"The executive Power shall be vested in a President of the United States of America."[48] That is to say, the entire executive power of the United States is given to one single person, the President. Since the president cannot do all that needs to be done, the Constitution allows him to delegate to staff and officers who assist him. Constitutionally, therefore, they act only under his authority. Officers and staff are extensions of the president and should speak and act as the president would speak and act. An officer or staff acting independently of the president is acting unconstitutionally. The notion of an independent head of department or an independent federal officer is contrary to Founding principles such as consent of the governed, a unitary executive, and representative government. Such a notion removes those officers from accountability to the people and places them outside any one of the three branches of constitutional government. The constitution allows for no fourth branch and no rogue officers or employees.

Choose candidates who support and defend the unitary executive.

EQUAL ENFORCEMENT OF THE LAW

The president should administer constitutional laws equally among all people regardless of the attempted influence of lobbyists, business executives, or other interest groups. If the American people do not like a law or its administration, the remedy is not to fail to administer the law, nor to pick and choose which groups have to follow the law and which do not. The executive should enforce constitutional law, and do so equally for everyone. Therefore, the people's just remedy for laws they do not like is to influence Congress to change the law. The media might rail against the executive's equally enforcing the law as written. Academics might rail against it. Interest groups may rail against it and sue. But it is the executive's duty to enforce constitutional law until Congress changes the law. It is the people's responsibility to ensure Congress acts on their wishes.

Choose candidates who promote equal enforcement of constitutional law.

Limited Power to Legislate

The original Constitution limited the powers of the federal government. It did this before any amendments were ratified, including the Bill of Rights. In fact, the very first section of the very first article of the Constitution, right after the Preamble, states, "All legislative Powers herein granted shall be vested in a Congress of the United States".[49] The wording tells us that out of the corpus of all legislative powers that exist or may exist, only certain legislative powers are granted to the federal government by the Constitution. It is as though, right up front, from the very beginning, the Founders wanted to be clear that the federal government could pass only certain types of laws.

Additionally, the Constitution tells us that laws must go through the U.S. Congress, "which shall consist of a Senate and House of Representatives," and that no bill, "Order, Resolution, or Vote" which both the House and Senate must pass, can take effect until one of three things happen. Either the President approves and signs the bill; or he objects to the bill and both houses of Congress pass the bill by a two-thirds vote; or the President fails to sign or object to the bill and returns it to Congress within ten days. Thus, no prescriptive order that requires or prohibits action of the American people at large and that imposes penalties for the breaking of the order can constitutionally be of just effect unless passed by both houses of Congress and submitted to the President for approval.[50]

Choose candidates who will act according to the constitutional limits of legislative power.

CONGRESS SHOULD LEGISLATE

The job and duty of Congress are to legislate according to just principles and within the bounds set forth by the Constitution. Congressmen and senators are not meant to be a body of overseers who spend their time investigating and judging the comings and goings of other members of government. Though they do have the authority to impeach and to try impeachment when needed, their primary role and responsibility are to pass laws that the executive branch then executes under the direction and authority of the president. Senators and congressional representatives are the ones who should pass rules governing conduct, while the president of the United States—with the help of others of his choosing—is to ensure laws are carried out and enforced.

Whereas the Constitution allows for multiple executive departments that should answer to the President, it mentions no such departments within the congressional branch. Even if one argued that the House or the Senate, or both, could delegate the origination of law to other congressional departments, the rules or regulations created by those departments would still need to be approved by at least a majority of both the House and the Senate and "be presented to the President of the United States."[51]

Choose candidates who defend the process by which laws must be passed in order to be constitutionally valid.

Legislation Is to Protect Individual Rights, Not Regulate Decisions

Laws that are just protect individual rights[52] and the rights of our nation. Federal legislation justly does this by providing for the general welfare and the common defense, neither favoring nor disfavoring specific groups, states, or individuals. The wording of all law, whether federal, state, or local, should be clear enough and short enough that those who are bound by it can understand it. And laws should be few enough that those bound by them can know, understand, and remember them. The Constitution limits what the national congress can legislate. All else should be legislated by the states (still respecting and protecting the rights of all individuals equally) or left to individuals to make their own daily choices. The Tenth Amendment is a reminder that some powers are specifically reserved to the people.

Choose candidates who know that laws are meant to protect and not to direct.

The Judiciary Should Adjudicate, Not Legislate

The Constitution specifically gives to the courts the authority to adjudicate the law. Judges cannot constitutionally make law, nor universalize their decisions, nor concoct edicts and command people as though they were kings commanding subjects what to do. Court interpretations of the law and of the Constitution are limited in their jurisdiction. Courts are to interpret the law only for the parties involved in a particular case and only for that specific case. The power of the court's decision does not constitutionally flow beyond that case and those parties.

While the federal courts have usurped legislative power, they have also given up some of their judicial power to legislative bodies and to regulatory agencies. By deferring to the opinions of regulatory agencies and to state legislative bodies, the courts abdicate their sacred responsibility to determine the constitutionality of law and to interpret law. There is no constitutional standard of "reasonable" or "intelligible" basis to which courts must defer. The court's role is not to determine if a state legislature had a good reason for its law or to determine if a regulatory agency had a reasonable interpretation of a law. Likewise, judges should not defer to judgments made in prior cases at the expense of making incorrect decisions today. While precedent is often followed, it is also broken by the Supreme Court, and sometimes broken even while the Court coyly says it is kept. Bad precedents should not be followed, and instead should be corrected.

Choose candidates who know that judges are to judge and not regulate.

Independent Judiciary Required

An independent judiciary is crucial to protecting the innocent, preserving and restoring liberty, and administering justice. Yet today, many cases are heard by judges who belong to the regulatory agency who made the rule, or rules, in question and who charged that an individual or group broke the rule the agency made. Not only is this a tyrannical combination of powers within one agency—something which is strictly contrary to liberty and to the principles of the Founding—it risks tremendous bias against those charged with breaking the law.

Choose candidates who will support an independent judiciary.

National Defense

One of the federal government's few authorized responsibilities is to provide for the common defense. George Washington said, "To be prepared for war is one of the most effectual means of preserving peace."[53] Our military, then, and its weapons and defensive equipment are of top priority. We should be continually innovating and developing equipment and methods of defense and of attack. We should preserve all American sovereignty in developing, testing, and manufacturing weapons and defensive technologies as will best defend our country and deter those who would be our enemies. Deregulating business and human life can unleash creativity and innovation, allowing us to better prepare and adapt for war. Deregulation also promotes economic prosperity which can provide the resources for research, development, manufacture, and purchase of military equipment.

Preparing for war and for attacks must be done with the understanding that each human life is precious, both the lives of our citizens and the lives of those who may seek to destroy or conquer us. We should therefore seek peace through all reasonable means, fighting only when necessary and right before God. We must be free of treaties that bind us to fight when it is not right to fight. And we must have the courage to fight when it is right.

In addition to a strong military and advanced technology, we must learn true principles of goodness and follow them. Abraham Lincoln stated that "Right makes might."[54] It does so because it pulls down the powers of heaven upon us. As true as there are laws of science that have existed since before we were born, there are laws of living that existed before we were born and that are independent of us. Power comes from following those laws. Even more power comes from learning about and worshiping the God who gave us the liberty we seek to protect.

Finally, we must know, love, and defend the fires of liberty and that which brings about and maintains liberty. Internal dissent, flattering and false philosophies, and the secret machinations of U.S. citizens willing to lie, steal and kill in order to gain and maintain power are better able to bring down our republic than the missiles and bombs of any foreign country.

Indeed, the pillars of security are (1) a strong and capable military with advanced technology and defensive structures, (2) maintenance of our nation's sovereignty, (3) freedom to take initiative and be creative, (4) a belief in the sacredness of all human life (4) moral living, (6) faithfulness to God, and (7) a united love of liberty.

Choose candidates who seek to prevent war and who promote the seven pillars of national security.

Fiscal Frugality

Except under extreme conditions such as war, the country should not enter into debt. We should reduce costs, live within our means, and pay back existing debts. Debt to foreign countries puts us in bondage and gives them undue influence. Until we have a surplus of money from which to draw, we should limit gifts to other countries. One area of cost reductions can come by returning to a three-branch system of government wherein Congress is the body that makes laws and the President authorizes them. In addition to reducing federal costs, this will ensure greater accountability to the people; help return us to government by consent of the governed; restore rights and opportunities; benefit our economy, and provide overall greater freedom for individuals. Another area of cost reductions is limiting the federal government's involvement in state and local affairs and leaving to them what should be left to them.

Choose candidates who believe our country should live within its means and get out of debt.

Privacy in the Public Sector: Government Should Not Be a Reality T.V. Show

The delegates to the 1787 Constitutional Convention met in private for four months. This teaches us a lesson in government. There must be a time of privacy so that open and free discussions can occur.

The conversations and writings of executive officers, their advisors, and aids must be held in utmost confidence. Executive officers and staff must be able to offer frank recommendations without fear of reprisal. Once a policy is made public, then the people can support or attack the policy as they will. But before then, recommendations, analyses, opinions, cabinet meetings, and diplomatic communications should be absolutely private and protected by law. People must have the freedom and confidence to express their thoughts and feelings freely and to have freedom to change their minds. This requires an assurance of privacy.

Confirmation hearings can be private. The Constitution states that the Senate must consent to the appointment of "Ambassadors, other public Ministers and Consuls, Judges of the supreme Court, and all other Officers of the United States, whose Appointments are not herein otherwise pro-vided for."[55] For major positions, this consent is now usually granted following a confirmation hearing. However, these hearings are not required.[56] Public confirmation hearings today can include merciless attacks and deliberate attempts to destroy reputation. This should not be. There is no need to publicly besmirch a person's reputation, regardless of party. If hearings are held, they should be private in order to respect the life and family of those being considered.

Choose candidates who believe government's purpose is not to provide soundbites, rumors, and headlines, but to protect lives and rights so people have a chance to live peacefully and happily.

PART 3

CALL TO ACTION: RECLAIMING OUR LIBERTY

"I know no safe depository of the ultimate powers of the society, but the people themselves: and if we think them not enlightened enough to exercise their control with a wholesome discretion, the remedy is, not to take it from them, but to inform their discretion by education. This is the true corrective of abuses of constitutional power." [57]

THOMAS JEFFERSON
To William Charles Jarvis
September 28, 1820

What can we do to reclaim our liberty?

1. Study the Constitution, the Declaration of Independence, and other documents of the Founding such as the Federalist papers. Learn the principles on which they are based. Seek for discernment to recognize which commentaries are historically accurate and which present a reinterpreta-

tion of history.

2. Remember God's miraculous and guiding hand in your life and in the life of this country. Express gratitude to God, thanking Him for family, for friends, for the freedom to speak your mind and provide for yourself. Thank him for the gift of life. Praise Him for being able to live in the United States and for the Constitution that provides great freedoms.

3. Commit to exercising your sovereignty and encourage others to do the same.

4. Share with others your commitment to self-government, personal responsibility, the equal protection of rights, and a government based on "the consent of the governed." Sign the pledge at FireofFreedom.org.

5. Gather together with other lovers of liberty and equality under the law. Host Gatherings of Liberty both virtually and in person (where allowed).

6. Encourage people to run for office who are both moral and wise, who understand and support principles of freedom and liberty, who will sustain and protect the Constitution of the United States, who put loyalty to the Constitution and to freedom before loyalty to party, who seek to unite rather than divide, and who will promote these principles. Find, promote, and elect candidates who support the standard of liberty and have the fire of freedom burning inside. Pray for your choice of candidate.

7. Promote the changing of state laws so that independents and minority-party candidates are treated equally to Democrat or Republican candidates with regards to getting onto ballots, and so that states will allow and honor all write-ins.

8. If people who are good candidates for any level of office are not listed on a ballot, encourage them to run as write-in candidates. Enlist the help of others to encourage

them as well. Your state may require that the candidate file as a write-in candidate by a certain time. Candidates for president may need to tell the state ahead of time who their electoral college electors are. Therefore, find people to be electors (in the electoral college) who will vote for your write-in candidate if he or she wins the state or district vote.

9. Don't re-elect people who violate the Constitution and our rights.

10. Work together regardless of political party.

11. Run for office yourself.

12. Share your opinion with friends and neighbors, with your governmental officers and representatives, and with non-elected officials who manage government.

13. Let the fire of freedom burn in you.

Now is the time to fulfill our responsibilities and reclaim our freedom and privileges. Let us lift the standard of liberty and fuel the fire of freedom!

*****

If you are committed to the principles of liberty and the Constitution, go to www.FireOfFreedom.com to sign the pledge or email Committed@FireOfFreedom.com.

*****

NOTES

1. Alexander Hamilton, John Jay, and James Madison, "No. 2," in *The Federalist*, Gideon Edition, ed., George W. Carey and James McClellan, (Indianapolis: Liberty Fund, 2001), 6. *The Federalist Papers* can also be readily found online at https://avalon.law.yale.edu/subject_menus/fed.asp or https://guides.loc.gov/federalist-papers/full-text. Quotations have been verified against the Gideon edition, but may have been originally copied from the yale.edu or other online source. Ideas cited from *The Federalist* may have come from the print or an online source or personal notes.

2. If there had not been the real threat of disunion, the authors of *The Federalist* would not have argued so fervently for Union and for the Constitution as the means of preserving that union. See papers 1-13, 15-20, and 23.

3. *Federalist*, "No. 1," 1.

4. *Federalist*, "No. 2," 7.

5. *Federalist*, "No. 15."

6. Editorial Note in "Vices of the Political System of the United States, April 1787," Founders Online, accessed 15 August 2020, https://founders.archives.gov/documents/Madison/01-09-02-0187.

7. In other words, the safety and peace of the people depended on UNION, and union depended on a better-formed government based on specific principles. See *The Federalist*,

as a whole.

8. "Road to the Constitution - Creating the United States | Exhibitions - Library of Congress," April 12, 2008, accessed August 27, 2020, www.loc.gov/exhibits/creating-the-united-states/road-to-the-constitution.html.

9. "States Which Seceded | EHISTORY," accessed August 27, 2020, ehistory.osu.edu/articles/states-which-seceded.

10. Guy Gugliotta, "New Estimate Raises Civil War Toll," *The New York Times*, April 2, 2012, accessed 22 August 2020, www.nytimes.com/2012/04/03/science/civil-war-toll-up-by-20-percent-in-new-estimate.html. See third-to-last paragraph.

11. Christine Hadlock, unpublished text and conversation(s), 2020.

12. Exodus 32:1 King James Version (KJV)

13. Exodus 32:4

14. 1 Samuel 10:18

15. John Jay, "The Founding Fathers on Jesus, Christianity and the Bible," 2016, WallBuilders, accessed August 15, 2020, https://wallbuilders.com/founding-fathers-jesus-christianity-bible/. John Jay, *The Correspondence and Public Papers of John Jay: 1794-1826*, vol. IV, ed. Henry P. Johnston, book digitized by Google, (New York: G. P. Putnam's Sons, 1890), 477. Accessed August 15, 2020, https://www.google.com/books/edition/_/K2UsAAAAIAAJ.

16. Christopher Columbus, ed., *Repertorium Columbianum, vol. 3, The Book of Prophecies*, historical and textual ed. Roberto Rusconi, trans. Blair Sullivan. (Berkeley: University of California Press), 67, 68, PDF on the website of Church of The Holy Family, accessed September 12, 2020, https://chfepiscopal.org/wp-content/uploads/2019/03/Columbus-Book-of-Prophecies.pdf. 1 Nephi 13:12, *The Book of Mormon: Another Testament of Jesus Christ*.

17. Peter A. Lillback with Jerry Newcombe, *George Washington's Sacred Fire.* (Bryn Mawr, PA: Providence Forum Press, 2006), 37, 578.

18. *Federalist*, "No. 37," 184, 185. James Madison, "The Finger of God on the Constitutional Convention," WallBuilders, 2017, accessed August 15, 2020, https://wallbuilders.com/finger-god-constitutional-convention/. (Note that the quote on WallBuilders adds an underline to three words and changes "a" to "the" before "finger.)(First words in quotations are from Rush, second set of words are from Franklin.)

19. Benjamin Rush and Benjamin Franklin, "The Finger of God on the Constitutional Convention," WallBuilders, 2017,accessed August 15, 2020, https://wallbuilders.com/finger-god-constitutional-convention/.

20. Abraham Lincoln, "Proclamation Appointing a National Fast Day," in *Collected Works of Abraham Lincoln*, vol. 6, The Abraham Lincoln Association, accessed August 15, 2020. quod.lib.umich.edu/cgi/t/text/text-idx?c=lincoln;rgn=div1;view=text;idno=lincoln6;node=lincoln6:336.

21. *Dred Scott v. Sandford*, 60 U.S. 393 (1856), Justia Law, accessed May 2, 2020. supreme.justia.com/cases/federal/us/60/393/. (Click on "Case")

22. There were other arguments as well.

23. William Harper, "Memoir on Slavery," in *The Ideology of Slavery: Proslavery Thought in the Antebellum South, 1830-1860*. ed. Drew Gilpin Faust (Baton Rouge: Louisiana State University Press, 1981), 85, 89.

24. Abraham Lincoln said,

"Will they be satisfied if the Territories be unconditionally surrendered to them? We know they will not. In all their present complaints against us, the Territories are scarcely mentioned. Invasions and insurrections are the rage now.

Will it satisfy them, if, in the future, we have nothing to do with invasions and insurrections? We know it will not. We so know, because we know we never had anything to do with invasions and insurrections; and yet this total abstaining does not exempt us from the charge and the denunciation.

The question recurs, what will satisfy them? Simply this: We must not only let them alone, but we must, somehow, convince them that we do let them alone. This, we know by experience, is no easy task. We have been so trying to convince them from the very beginning of our organization, but with no success. In all our platforms and speeches we have constantly protested our purpose to let them alone; but this has had no tendency to convince them. Alike unavailing to convince them, is the fact that they have never detected a man of us in any attempt to disturb them.

These natural, and apparently adequate means all failing, what will convince them? This, and this only: cease to call slavery wrong, and join them in calling it right. And this must be done thoroughly---done in acts as well as in words. Silence will not be tolerated---we must place ourselves avowedly with them. Senator Douglas's new sedition law must be enacted and enforced, suppressing all declarations that slavery is wrong, whether made in politics, in presses, in pulpits, or in private. We must arrest and return their fugitive slaves with greedy pleasure. We must pull down our Free State constitutions. The whole atmosphere must be disinfected from all taint of opposition to slavery, before they will cease to believe that all their troubles proceed from us."

Abraham Lincoln, "Address at Cooper Institute, New York City," in *Collected Works of Abraham Lincoln*, vol. 3, The Abraham Lincoln Association, accessed August 17, 2020, https://quod.lib.umich.edu/l/lincoln/lincoln3/1:199?

rgn=div1;view=fulltext.

Lincoln did not use the term "positive good," in this speech. John C. Calhoun used the term in a speech on February 6, 1837,

"But I take higher ground. I hold that in the present state of civilization, where two races of different origin, and distinguished by color, and other physical differences, as well as intellectual, are brought together, the relation now existing in the slaveholding States between the two, is, instead of an evil, a good–a positive good."

John C. Calhoun, "Slavery a Positive Good," Teaching American History, accessed 17 August 2020, https://teachingamericanhistory.org/library/document/slavery-a-positive-good/.

25. "Declaration of Independence: A Transcription," National Archives, accessed October 14, 2020, www.archives.gov/founding-docs/declaration-transcript. (Capitalization changed.)
26. United States Constitution, art. I § 1, https://www.archives.gov/founding-docs/constitution-transcript.
27. 1 Samuel 9:2
28. 1 Samuel 13:14 and Acts 13:22
29. 1 Kings 3:12
30. *Federalist*, "No. 51," 269.
31. *Federalist*, "No. 47," 249.
32. Alexander Hamilton, *Federalist*, "No. 9," 38.
33. U.S. Const. art. II § 1.
34. Declaration of Independence.
35. United States Constitution, art. VI. https://www.archives.gov/founding-docs/constitution-transcript. See also

U.S. Const. art. II § 1. 5 U.S. Code § 3331 - Oath of Office, Legal Information Institute, Cornell Law School, accessed September 1, 2020, https://www.law.cornell.edu/uscode/text/5/3331.

36. John Adams, "From John Adams to Massachusetts Militia, 11 October 1798," Founders Online, National Archives, accessed August 17, 2020, https://founders.archives.gov/documents/Adams/99-02-02-3102.

37. U.S. Const. art. IV, § 4.

38. U.S. Const. art. II, § 1.

39. U.S. Const. art. II, § 3.

40. U.S. Const. art. VI.

41. U.S. Const. art. VI.

42. Thomas Jefferson discusses this idea in his letter to William H. Torrance, June 11, 1815. Thomas Jefferson, "Thomas Jefferson to William H. Torrance, 11 June 1815," Founders Online, National Archives, accessed August 15, 2020, https://founders.archives.gov/documents/Jefferson/03-08-02-0427. [Original source: *The Papers of Thomas Jefferson*, Retirement Series, vol. 8, *1 October 1814 to 31 August 1815*, ed. J. Jefferson Looney. Princeton: Princeton University Press, 2011, pp. 524–528.]

43. U.S. Const. art. III, § 2. https://www.archives.gov/founding-docs/constitution-transcript.

44. *Marbury v Madison*, 5. U.S. 137 (1803). https://supreme.justia.com/cases/federal/us/5/137/#tab-opinion-1958607

45. *Marbury v Madison*.

46. Thomas Jefferson, "Thomas Jefferson to William Charles Jarvis, 28 September 1820," Founders Online, National Archives, accessed August 15, 2020, https://founders.archives.gov/documents/Jefferson/98-01-02-1540, (Early access document). (Capitalization added.)

47. Five years earlier, Jefferson wrote:

"The ... question whether the judges are invested with exclusive authority to decide on the constitutionality of a law, has been heretofore a subject of consideration with me in the exercise of official duties. [C]ertainly there is not a word in the constitution which has given that power to them more than to the Executive or Legislative branches."

Jefferson, "Thomas Jefferson to William H. Torrance, 11 June 1815."

48. U.S. Const. art. II, § 1.
49. U.S. Const. art. I, § 1.
50. U.S. Const. art. I, § 7.
51. U.S. Const. art. I, § 7.
52. Frederic Bastiat wrote,

"It is not true that the function of law is to regulate our consciences, our ideas, our wills, our education, our opinions, our work, our trade, our talents, or our pleasures. The function of law is to protect the free exercise of these rights, and to prevent any person from interfering with the free exercise of these same rights by any other person."

Frederic Bastiat, "The Law," Foundation for Economic Freedom (FEE), November 16, 2012, accessed September 12, 2020. https://fee.org/resources/the-law/.

53. George Washington, "From George Washington to the United States Senate and House of Representatives, 8 January 1790," Founders Online, National Archives, https://founders.archives.gov/documents/Washington/05-04-02-0361. [Original source: *The Papers of George Washington, Presidential Series, vol. 4, 8 September 1789*

– 15 January 1790, ed. Dorothy Twohig. Charlottesville: University Press of Virginia, 1993, pp. 543–549.]

54. Lincoln, Abraham. "Address at Cooper Institute, New York City."

55. U.S. Const. art. 2, § 2.

56. "Nominations: A Historical Overview," United States Senate, https://www.senate.gov/artandhistory/history/common/briefing/Nominations.htm.

57. Jefferson, "Thomas Jefferson to William Charles Jarvis, 28 September 1820." (Capitalization and spelling modernized.)